PUFFIN BOOKS
UK I USA I Australia I Canada I India I Ireland I New Zealand I South Africa
Puffin Books is part of the Penguin Random House group of companies
whose addresses can be found at global.penguinrandomhouse.com.
puffinbooks.com

First published 2016
001

ISBN 978–0–141–36853–5

To find out more about Eric Carle and his books, please visit eric-carle.com
To learn about The Eric Carle Museum of Picture Book Art,
please visit carlemuseum.org

CALM

WITH THE VERY HUNGRY CATERPILLAR

Eric Carle

PUFFIN

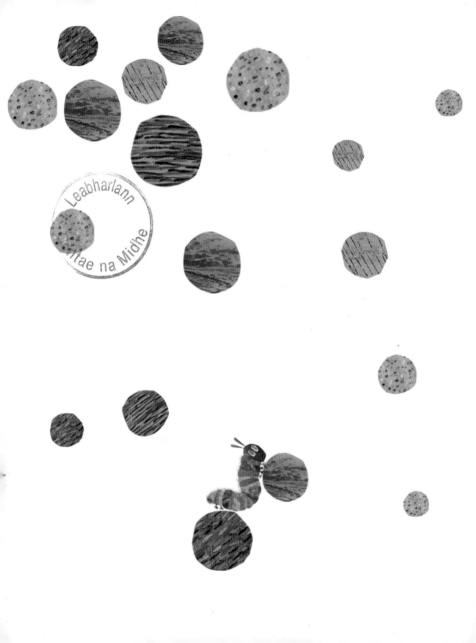

When **your . . .**

monkey mind

feels too busy...

just stop and
breathe…

to clear the
cobwebs
from your head.

With each slow breath, try counting

from 1 to 10.

How do you feel?

Jumpy?

calm?

Now let thoughts cross your mind

like

clouds

floating in the sky.

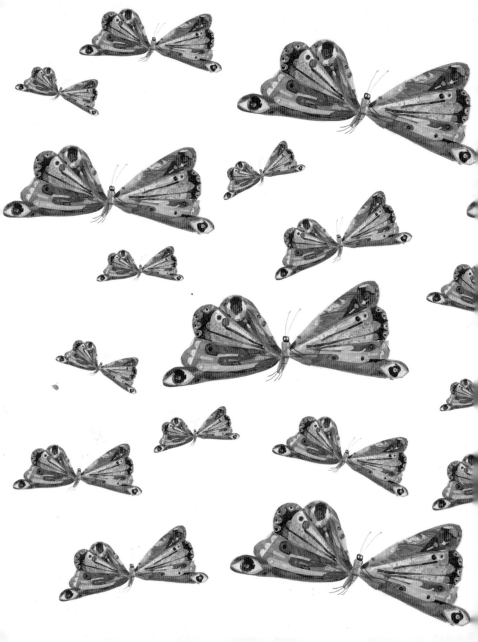

Still feeling

fluttery?

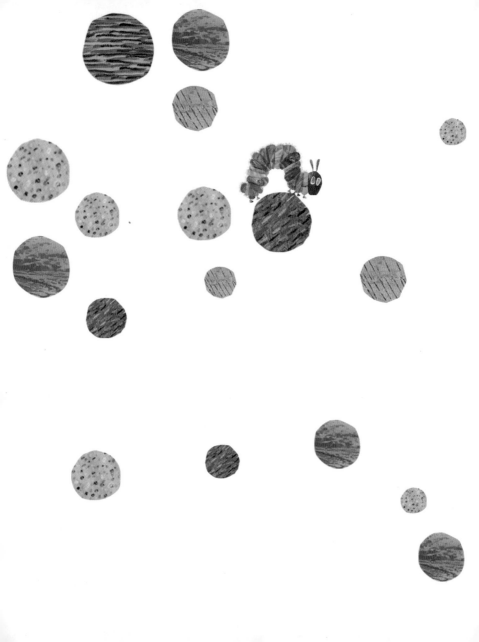

Take a few
deep
breaths...

and

SMILE!

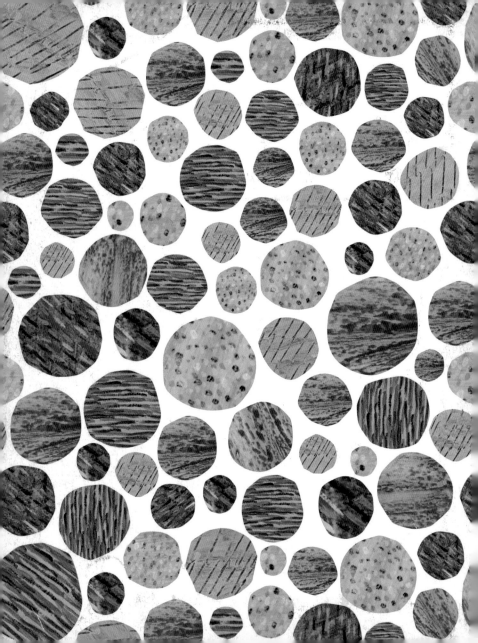